AF269745

Lerner SPORTS

ALL-STAR
SMACK
DOWN

TIGER WOODS VS. JACK NICKLAUS

WHO WOULD WIN?

K.C. KELLEY

Lerner Publications ◆ Minneapolis

Lerner Publications Company
An imprint of Lerner Publishing Group, Inc.
241 First Avenue North
Minneapolis, MN 55401 USA

For reading levels and more information, look up this title at www.lernerbooks.com.

Main body text set in Aptifer Sans LT Pro.
Typeface provided by Linotype AG.

Library of Congress Cataloging-in-Publication Data

Names: Kelley, K. C, author.
Title: Tiger Woods vs. Jack Nicklaus : who would win? / K.C. Kelley.
Description: Minneapolis, MN : Lerner Publications, [2025] | Series: All-star smackdown | Includes bibliographical references and index. | Audience: Ages 7–11 | Audience: Grades 4–6 | Summary: "Combined, golf superstars Tiger Woods and Jack Nicklaus have won an incredible 33 major championships. Many fans believe they're the best ever. But which golfer is better? Compare their careers and make your own decision"— Provided by publisher.
Identifiers: LCCN 2023042582 (print) | LCCN 2023042583 (ebook) | ISBN 9798765625910 (library binding) | ISBN 9798765628157 (paperback) | ISBN 9798765632246 (epub)
Subjects: LCSH: Woods, Tiger,—Juvenile literature. | Nicklaus, Jack,—Juvenile literature. | Golfers—United States—Biography—Juvenile literature. | Golf—United States—Juvenile literature. | Professional Golfers' Association of America—Juvenile literature.
Classification: LCC GV964.W66 K45 2025 (print) | LCC GV964.W66 (ebook) | DDC 796.352092 [B]—dc23/eng/20230912

LC record available at https://lccn.loc.gov/2023042582
LC ebook record available at https://lccn.loc.gov/2023042583

Manufactured in the United States of America
1 – CG – 7/15/24

TABLE OF CONTENTS

INTRODUCTION

TWO GOLF GREATS

On April 13, 1997, Tiger Woods walked slowly up the 18th fairway at Augusta National Golf Club in Augusta, Georgia. Fans surrounding the green ahead of him stood and cheered.

>> Fast Facts <<

-  Tiger Woods has won golf's major tournaments 15 times. The majors are the Masters, the US Open, the British Open, and the PGA Championship.
- Woods was the Professional Golfers' Association (PGA) Player of the Year 11 times.
- Jack Nicklaus won 18 major tournaments.
- Nicklaus was the PGA Player of the Year five times.

At 21, Woods was about to win the Masters by 12 strokes. It was the start of a great golf career.

When he won the 1997 Masters, Woods was already a US amateur and college champion. After winning the Masters, he became one of the most famous athletes on the planet. The Masters was the first of 15 major tournaments he won.

Jack Nicklaus, with 18 major titles, is the only player with more major wins than Woods. Nicklaus was also a young golf superstar. He was only 22 when he won his first major at the US Open in 1962. As Woods would do years later, Nicklaus became the best golfer in the world.

Jack Nicklaus

Woods was a world champion before he was ten years old. Nicklaus became a star as a teenage amateur. Woods played college golf, and so did Nicklaus. One of the best parts of Woods's game was his long drives. Nicklaus also was a powerful player, thrilling fans with big hits.

Nicklaus set the standard, winning more majors and honors than any other golfer. Woods continues to pursue Nicklaus's records, but many think Woods is already the better player. Who do you think is better? Let the smackdown begin!

Nicklaus won his third British Open trophy in 1978.

Woods burst onto
the golf scene
when he was only
21 and became
one of the most
famous athletes
in the world.

CHAPTER 1

Jack Nicklaus (left) and his father, L. C. Nicklaus (right), after Jack won the 1953 National Junior Golf Tournament

THE ROAD TO THE PGA TOUR

Jack Nicklaus was born January 21, 1940, in Ohio. He played many sports when he was young, including basketball, tennis, and track. When he was 10, he started playing golf. It quickly became his favorite sport. By the age of 12, he was the Ohio state junior champion. Four years later, he won a state tournament open to golfers of all ages.

Nicklaus won 27 trophies in Ohio as a teenage golfer. When he was 16, he earned a spot in the 1957 US Open. After graduating from high school, he went to nearby Ohio State University.

Nicklaus quickly showed that he was one of the country's best young golfers. He was the US Amateur champion in 1959 and 1961. In 1961, Nicklaus became the first player to win both the amateur and college championships in the same year.

Nicklaus blasts the ball out of a sand trap on his way to winning the 1961 US Amateur Championship.

Nicklaus shows off his awards after winning the 1961 national college championship.

Nicklaus joined the PGA Tour in 1961. His first pro victory came in the 1962 US Open. After four rounds, Nicklaus was tied with Arnold Palmer. At the time, Palmer was the most famous PGA pro. His millions of fans called themselves Arnie's Army.

Nicklaus beat Palmer in a playoff to win the Open. The young golfer began a long rivalry with Palmer, and the two became great friends. Together, they were the best in golf for most of the 1960s.

Nicklaus watches his ball during the 1962 US Open.

CONSIDER THIS

Nicklaus earned $17,500 for his 1962 US Open victory. In 2000, Woods won his first US Open. He earned $800,000 for the win. The 2023 winner, Wyndham Clark, earned $3.6 million.

Eldrick "Tiger" Woods was born on December 30, 1975, near Los Angeles, California. His father, Earl Woods, loved golf. Tiger followed his dad around, swinging tiny clubs. Soon after he turned two years old, Tiger was on TV, showing off his swing.

Tiger was only eight years old when he won the first of six Junior World Golf Championships. At 15, he became the youngest winner ever at the US Junior Amateur Championship. He later was the first to win the US Amateur Championship three years in a row, from 1994 to 1996.

Tiger Woods (left) and Earl Woods (right) with the 1991 US Junior Amateur trophy.

Since his early days in golf, Woods has always worn a red shirt on the final Sunday of a tournament.

Some people focused on the color of Woods's skin. They compared him to great Black golfers such as Charlie Sifford and Lee Elder. Woods was honored, but he didn't want to be known as only a Black golfer. He wanted to be the best golfer. Soon, his popularity helped attract many new fans and players to golf.

In 1994, Woods entered Stanford University. He became an All-American and won the men's college golf national title. He turned pro in 1996.

After winning two tournaments in his first pro season, Woods earned the 1996 PGA Tour Rookie of the Year award. In April 1997, he won the Masters, his first major title. By the summer of 1997, he was the number one golfer in the world.

Woods smiles
while speaking to
fans after he won
the 1997 Masters.

CHAPTER 2

Nicklaus makes his final shot at the 1965 Masters.

GREATEST MOMENTS

By the early 1960s, Nicklaus was one of the top pro golfers. He won his first Masters in 1963. That year, he also won the PGA Championship, another major event. At the 1965 Masters, Nicklaus was tied with Arnold Palmer and Gary Player after two rounds. In the third round, Nicklaus shot a 65 to take the lead. By the end of the fourth and final round, Nicklaus had won by a record nine strokes. His total of 271 strokes was a Masters all-time best.

Nicklaus continued winning throughout the 1960s. In 1966, he won his first British Open. That gave him one win in each of the four majors. Winning all four majors is a Grand Slam. Only six male golfers have ever completed the Grand Slam. Nicklaus did it only five years into his PGA career.

CONSIDER THIS

Nicklaus's nickname is The Golden Bear. It comes from his blond hair and high school mascot. Woods's nickname, Tiger, was the nickname of one of his father's friends in the US Army.

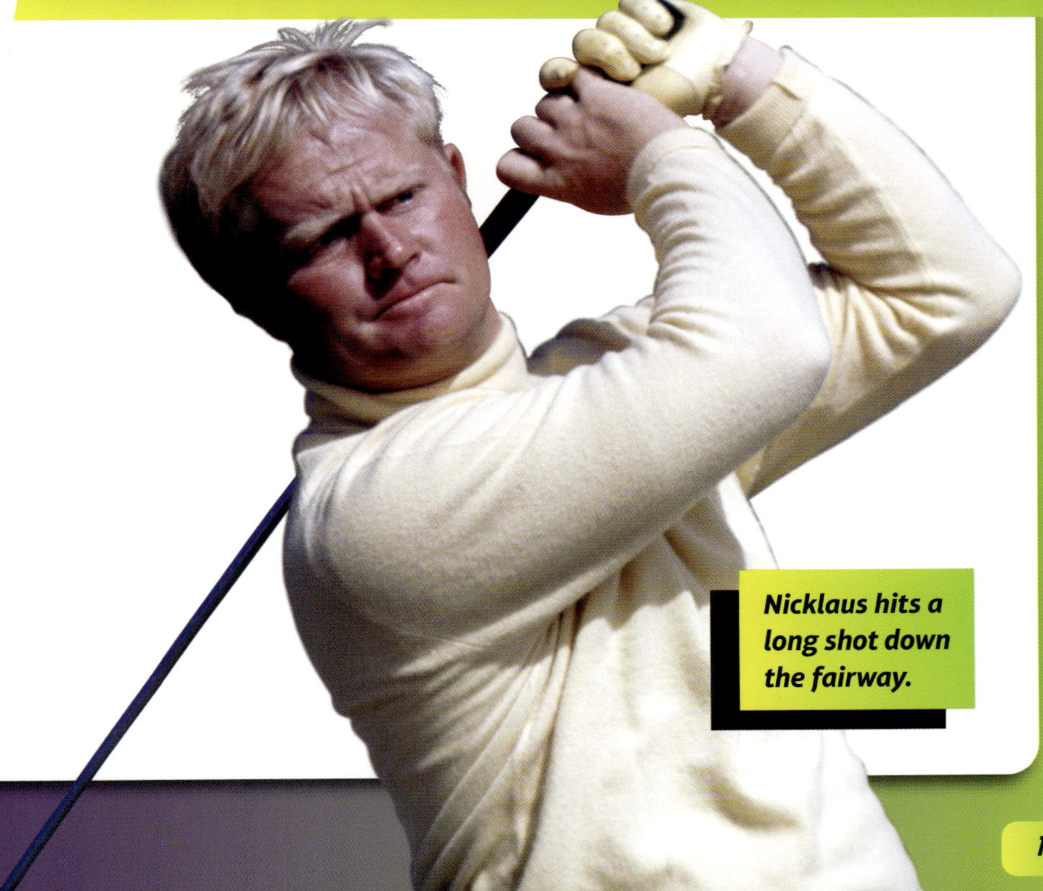

Nicklaus hits a long shot down the fairway.

In 1997, Woods broke several of Nicklaus's Masters records. Wearing a red shirt as he always did for the final round, Woods made birdie after birdie. The young golfer pumped his fist with joy after making big shots. He amazed opponents with his ability to hit any shot. His 12-stroke win topped Nicklaus's biggest Masters wins. Woods's final score of 270 also beat Nicklaus's 1965 score.

Woods became known for his leg-kicking, fist-pumping celebrations of big putts.

Woods held up the trophy at the 2008 US Open, an event he has won three times.

In 2000, Woods led the PGA Tour with nine wins. He won the US Open, the British Open, and the PGA Championship to complete the Grand Slam. Like Nicklaus, it had taken Woods only five years to do it.

The rest of the 2000s belonged to Woods. He added nine more major titles through 2009. He was the PGA Player of the Year and the PGA Tour's top money winner eight times from 1999 to 2009.

CHAPTER 3

RECORD-SETTING SEASONS

In the 1970s, golf belonged to Jack Nicklaus. He won 38 PGA Tour events and eight majors. He was the top money winner five times. He also won five PGA Player of the Year awards.

Nicklaus was still active and successful when he joined the World Golf Hall of Fame in 1974. This honor is usually for players who have retired. In 1976, Nicklaus created his own PGA event, The Memorial. It is still held every year in Columbus, Ohio, his hometown.

In 1986, Nicklaus had one more moment at the top. He had not won a major event in six years. But he shot 65 during the final round at the Masters and became a champion for the 18th time. Fans around the world were thrilled as he put on the green jacket, the symbol of the Masters winner. At 46, he was the oldest player to win the Masters.

Nicklaus puts on the green jacket at the 1986 Masters.

CONSIDER THIS

Nicklaus's 1986 Masters win gave him six green jackets in his career. Woods has won the famous event five times.

Woods began battling injuries in 2010. He hurt his back, his elbow, his neck, and his left leg. The injuries took away some of the power of his swing. But a determined Woods fought his way back to the course.

In 2013, he won five times and was again ranked number one in the world. He also helped the US win the Presidents Cup, an event featuring teams from countries around the world.

Like Nicklaus, Woods had a famous Masters victory late in his career. He returned to the Masters in 2019. Though often in pain from his injuries, he made shot after shot. On the final day, he walked up the 18th fairway to cheers from the crowd. At 43, Woods became the second oldest Masters winner ever, after Nicklaus.

Woods shouts for joy after making his final shot at the 2019 Masters.

CHAPTER 4

Woods (center) smiles with students from his learning center after he won a tournament in 2008.

AND THE WINNER IS

In this golf showdown, who finishes first? Both golfers piled up trophy after trophy. Who would win if they played each other at their best? That's for you to decide!

Both have used their fame to help others. The Tiger Woods Foundation helps children experience golf. Woods also built a learning center in Anaheim, California, that helps thousands of students. In 2019, he earned the Presidential Medal of Freedom for his charity work.

Nicklaus and his wife support children's medical charities in Ohio and Florida. His Memorial Tournament raises money for a children's hospital. In 2005, he also won the Presidential Medal of Freedom.

In 2012, Woods passed Nicklaus with his 74th PGA Tour win. Woods is tied for first place with Sam Snead with 82 wins. Woods also has earned more than $120 million in prize money, far more than any other player has. Modern golfers are paid much more than golfers earned when Nicklaus played.

President George W. Bush presents Nicklaus with the Presidential Medal of Freedom.

Experts and fans think there are more great golfers today than ever before. Did Nicklaus play against as many great players as Woods did?

Both golfers are the only players to have won three career Grand Slams. They are first and second all-time in major title wins. Both are in the World Golf Hall of Fame.

Tiger Woods is our winner. His popularity, many major wins, and powerful style helped golf grow around the world. Who do you think the winner should be? Compare the stats and make your own choice!

Nicklaus (right) presented the trophy to Woods (left) when Woods won the 2012 Memorial tournament.

27

TIGER WOODS

Date of birth: December 30, 1975
PGA Player of the Year awards: 11
Major championships: 14
Total PGA wins: 82

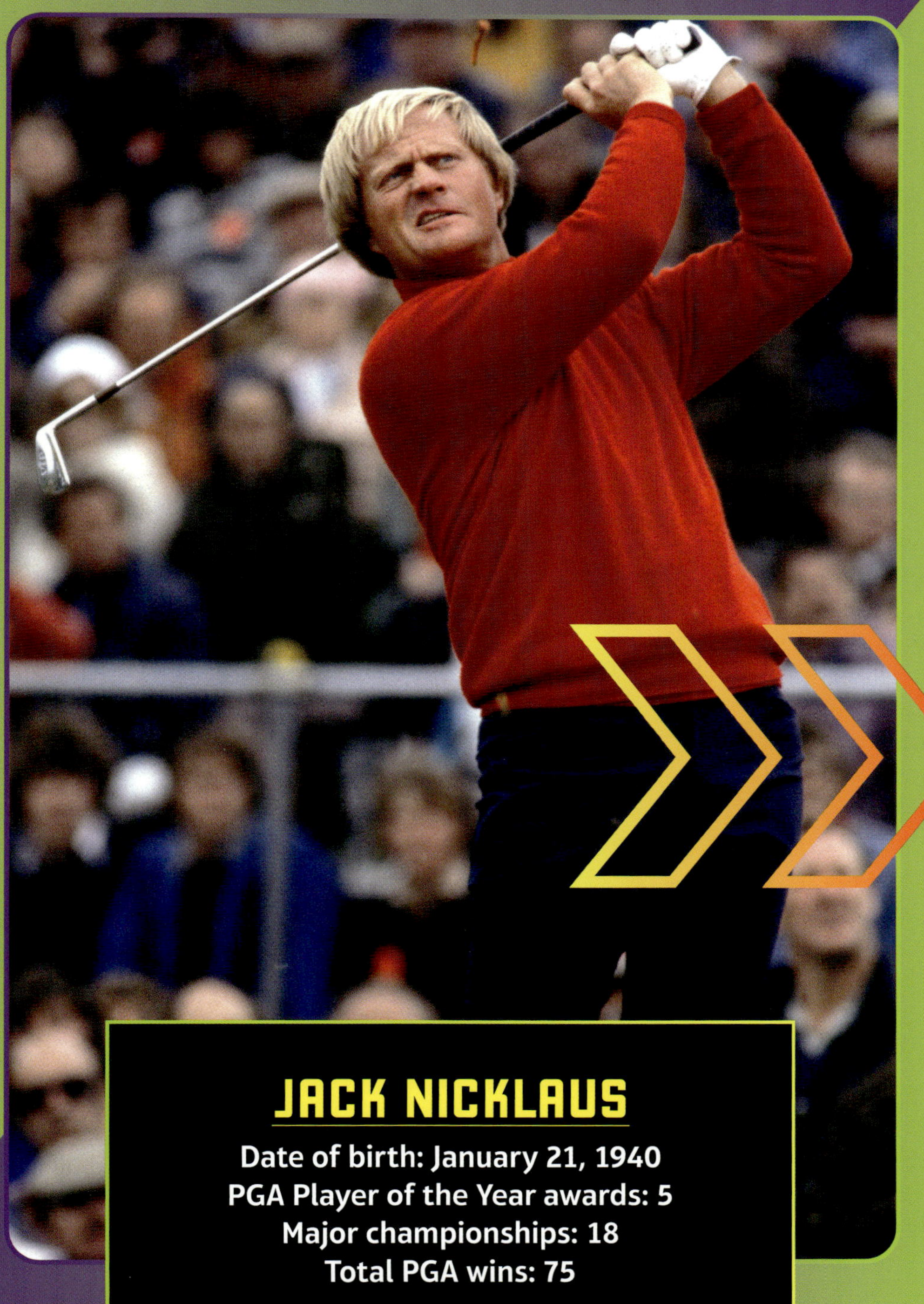

JACK NICKLAUS
Date of birth: January 21, 1940
PGA Player of the Year awards: 5
Major championships: 18
Total PGA wins: 75

GLOSSARY

All-American: one of the top players in a US college sport

amateur: playing a sport without being paid

birdie: a golf score of one stroke less than par on a hole

drive: when a golfer hits the ball from a tee

fairway: the mowed grassy area between a golf tee and the green

Grand Slam: winning all four major PGA tournaments

green: a smooth grassy area on a golf course that contains the hole

mascot: a person, animal, or object used as a symbol to represent a sports team and to bring good luck

PGA Tour: the top level of pro golf in the United States, played mainly by men

rivalry: when a player or team tries to defeat or be more successful than another

stroke: a golf swing

LEARN MORE

Brittanica Kids: Golf
https://kids.britannica.com/kids/article/golf/353194

Fishman, Jon M. *Golf's G.O.A.T.: Jack Nicklaus, Tiger Woods, and More.* Minneapolis: Lerner Publications, 2022.

Leed, Percy. *Tiger Woods: Major Winner.* Minneapolis: Lerner Sports, 2023.

PGA Jr. League
https://www.pgareach.org/services/youth

Sports Illustrated Kids: Golf
https://www.sikids.com/tag/golf

Williams, Doug. *Tiger Woods: Golf Legend.* North Mankato, MN: North Star Editions, 2018.

INDEX

PHOTO ACKNOWLEDGMENTS

Rob Schumacher-USA TODAY Sports, p 4; Eileen Blass/USA TODAY Network, p. 5; Mirrorpix/Newscom, p. 6; Scott A. Miller/ZUMA Press/Newscom, p. 7; AP Photo, p. 8; AP Photo, p. 9; AP Photo, p. 10; Bettmann/Getty Images, p. 11; Rick Dole/Getty Images, p. 12; AP Photo/Jack Smith, p. 13; AP Photo/ Mark Humphrey, p. 14; The Augusta Chronicle-USA TODAY Network, p. 15; Bettmann/Getty Images, p. 16; Ed Lacey/Popperphoto/Getty Images, p. 17; Porter Binks-USA TODAY Network, p. 18; Mark J. Rebilas-USA TODAY Sports, p. 19; Malcolm Emmons-USA TODAY Sports, p. 20; Porter Binks-USA TODAY NETWORK, p. 21; AP Photo/Darron Cummings, p. 22; Rob Schumacher-USA TODAY Sports, p. 23; AP Photo/Denis Poroy, p. 24; AP Photo/Lawrence Jackson, p. 25; Jason Mowry/Icon SMI/Newscom, p. 26; Michael Madrid-USA TODAY Sports, p. 27; Matthew Emmons- USA TODAY, p. 28; Leo Mason/Action Plus/Newscom, p. 29.

Cover: Chris O'Meara/AP Photo (Woods); The Augusta Chronicle via USA TODAY Network (Nicklaus)